LES TROIS
COCHONS

LES TROIS COCHONS

By Sheila Hébert Collins

Illustrated by Patrick Soper

PELICAN PUBLISHING COMPANY

Gretna 1999

With love and appreciation to my husband, Dennis,
my son, Cooper, and my daughter, Cody

First published by Blue Heron Press, 1995
Revised and published by arrangement with the author by
  Pelican Publishing Company, Inc., 1999

First Pelican edition, 1999

The word "Pelican" and the depiction of a pelican are trademarks
of Pelican Publishing Company, Inc., and are registered
in the U.S. Patent and Trademark Office.

Library of Congress Cataloging-in-Publication Data
Collins, Sheila Hébert.
  Les Trois Cochons / by Sheila Hébert Collins ; illustrated by
Patrick Soper
    p. cm.
    SUMMARY: A Cajun retelling of the familiar tale about three pigs who
set out to build homes of their own in Louisiana and then must outsmart a
hungry wolf. Includes pronunciation and definitions for the many French
words used in the story.
    ISBN 1-56554-325-4 (hardcover : alk. paper)
    I. Soper, Patrick, ill. II. Three little pigs. English. III.
Title.
    PZ8.1.C696 Tr 1999
    398.24'5296336—dc21   99-25569
                                                        CIP

Printed in Korea

Published by Pelican Publishing Company, Inc.
1000 Burmaster Street, Gretna, Louisiana 70053

LES TROIS COCHONS

Once upon a time, there was a family of *cochons* who lived near *Big Mamou* in southwest Louisiana. *Mamère Cochon* was so poor that she could no longer keep her *trois cochons* at home.

"You must go out into the world, *mes enfants*, and seek your fortune," *Mamère Cochon* sadly said one day.

She made them each a little *goûter* and kissed them goodbye. "*Bonne chance, ma famille, au revoir!*"

cochon (ko shon)—pig
Big Mamou (big mahmoo)—a small town in southwest Louisiana
Mamère (mah mare)—mother
trois (traw)—three
mes enfants (may zahn fahn)—my children
goûter (goo tay)—little taste of food
Bonne chance (bohn shans)—good luck
ma famille (mah fahmeal)—my family
au revoir (oh revwah)—good-bye

As soon as *les trois cochons* were out of their *mamère's* sight, they sat down for a little *tête à tête*.

"*Mais, jamais!* What will we do?" asked 'Ti Joe, the first *cochon*.

'Ti Claude, the second *cochon*, spoke up quickly. "*Mais*, I'm going to Crowley, me! Dat's where I'll have my fill of rice all day!"

"Not me, *chère!*" said 'Ti Frère, the third *cochon*. "I'm going to Abbeville, where I can get all dat sugarcane and sweet cane syrup I have an *envie* for."

tête à tête (tet ah tet)—private talk
Mais, jamais (mehn, zha may)—well, good grief
'Ti (tea)—short for petite (little)
chère (sha)—darling
'Ti Frère (tee frair)—little brother
envie (ohn vee)—a craving

"*Tu m'dis pas!*" said 'Ti Joe. "I can already smell dat good crawfish pie! Me, I'm going to *Breaux Bridge*, where I can eat all dat crawfish I want. But let's all meet in *Big Mamou* for the *Courir du Mardi Gras*. Until den, *mes frères,* watch out for dat *loup-garou*. He's been planning a *cochon du lait* for quite some time now, and would surely like to start with us! *Prend garde! Au revoir!*"

Tu m'dis pas (toom dee pah)—you don't say
Breaux Bridge (bro brij)—a town in southwest Louisiana
Courir du Mardi Gras (Coor eer doo Mar dee Grah)—running of the
 Mardi Gras, a custom in rural areas on Mardi Gras Day that involves
 running after chickens to make gumbo
mes frères (may frairs)—my brothers
loup-garou (loo gahroo)—wolf
cochon du lait (ko shohn doo lay)—pig roast
Prend garde (prohn gahrd)—be careful

Near Abbeville, 'Ti Frère met a man in a cane truck. "*Monsieur,* may I have some of dat sugarcane to build my house, *s'il vous plait?*"

"*Mais, oui,*" said the sugarcane farmer.

Then 'Ti Frère built a fine sugarcane house. *Avant longtemps,* the *loup-garou* came knocking at his door.

"'Ti Cochon, 'Ti Cochon, let me come in!" he said.

"*Non! Non! Non!*" said 'Ti Frère. "Not by the hair of my chinny chin, chin! *Laissez-moi tranquille!*"

Monsieur (m'syuhr)—mister
s'il vous plait (seal voo play)—if you please
Mais, oui (mehn, we)—well, yes
Avant longtemps (ah vohn lohn tohn)—before long
Non (nohn)—no
Laissez-moi tranquille (lay say mwah tron keel)—leave me alone

"*Ça c'est dommage!* Den I'll huff, and I'll puff, and I'll blow your house in!" said the *loup-garou*. So he huffed, and he puffed, and he blew that house in!

As his sugarcane house was falling down, 'Ti Frère ran out the back door and headed for Crowley.

"*Enfin!*" 'Ti Frère thought to himself. "Dat *loup-garou* won't have me for his *cochon du lait!*"

Ça c'est dommage (sah say dohn mahj)—that's too bad
Enfin (ohn fehn)—but really

The second *cochon*, 'Ti Claude, had just reached Crowley. There he found the biggest rice field he could. He met the rice farmer and asked, *"Monsieur,* may I have some rice stalks to build my house, *s'il vous plait?"*

"Mais, oui," said the rice farmer.

'Ti Claude gathered up the rice stalks and made a fine house.

Avant longtemps, the *loup-garou* came knocking at the door.
"'Ti Cochon, 'Ti Cochon, let me come in!" said the *loup-garou.*
"*Non! Non! Non!*" said 'Ti Claude. "Not by the hair of my chinny chin, chin! *Laissez-moi tranquille!*"

"*Ça c'est dommage!* Den I'll huff, and I'll puff, and I'll blow your rice-stalk house in!" yelled the *loup-garou*. Then he huffed, and he puffed, and he blew that rice-stalk house in! Just as 'Ti Claude's house was falling down, he ran out the back door, straight toward *Breaux Bridge.*

"*Enfin!*" 'Ti Claude thought to himself. "Dat *loup-garou* won't make *gratons* out of me!"

gratons (grah tohns)—fried pigskin

'Ti Joe had the longest trip to make . . . all the way to *Breaux Bridge*. But as he would always say, *"Vouloir c'est pouvoir."*

Near *Breaux Bridge,* 'Ti Joe met a man hauling oyster shells. "What a strong house dat would make," he thought.

Vouloir c'est pouvoir (voo wah say poov wah)—where there's a will, there's a way

"*Monsieur*, may I have some oyster shells to build my house, *s'il vous plait?*" asked 'Ti Joe.

"*Mais, oui*," said the man. "Where do you want dem?"

"*Là-bas, monsieur*, next to dat big crawfish pond," answered 'Ti Joe.

Then 'Ti Joe unloaded his oyster shells and began building his house with pond mud and oyster shells.

Là-bas (lah bah)—over there

Avant longtemps the *loup-garou* came knocking at his door.
"Ti Cochon, 'Ti Cochon, let me come in!" he yelled.
"*Non! Non! Non!*" said 'Ti Joe. "Not by the hair of my chinny
chin, chin! *Laissez-moi tranquille!*"

"*Ça c'est dommage!* Den I'll huff, and I'll puff, and I'll blow your oyster house in!" yelled the *loup-garou*. So he huffed, and he puffed, and he puffed, and he huffed, but he could never blow that strong oyster house down.

Having *le savoir-faire*, the *loup-garou* spoke up. "'Ti Cochon, I know where dere's a nice patch of *mirliton* vines."

"*Tu m'dis pas!* And where would dat be?" asked 'Ti Joe.

"In *Madame Dubois'* field. *Tu tiens d'y aller?*" asked the *loup-garou*.

"*Mais, bien sûr!* What time will you come for me?" asked 'Ti Joe.

"*De bon matin, à six heures,*" replied the *loup-garou*.

"*C'est bien!*" agreed 'Ti Joe.

le savoir-faire (ler sah vwah fair)—the know-how

mirliton (mer lee tohn)—vegetable pear

Madame Dubois (mah dahm doo bwah)—Mrs. / Cajun family name

Tu tiens d'y aller (too tyehn dah aly)—Do you wish to go?

Mais, bien sûr (mehn bee-ehn sur)—well, certainly

De bon matin, à six heures (Der bohn mah tehn, ah seez-er)—early in the morning, at six o'clock

C'est bien (say bee-ehn)— it's fine

The next morning that *canaille cochon* got up *à cinq heures* and went to *Madame Dubois'* field, picked his *mirlitons,* and came home.

À six heures, the *loup-garou* knocked at the door. "Are you ready?" he asked.

"*Ah-ee! Allez-vous-en, loup-garou!* I've already been to *Madame Dubois'* field and I'm boiling doz good *mirlitons* right now!" 'Ti Joe said.

canaille (kahn eye)—mischievous
À cinq heures (ah sank-r)—at five o'clock
Ah-ee (ah ee)—a Cajun saying (more like a howl or yell)
Allez-vous-en (ah lay voo-zohn)—go away

The *loup-garou* was *bien fâché* when he heard this, but he was determined not to be outsmarted by that *cochon,* so he said, "'Ti Cochon, I know where there's a beautiful fig tree loaded with ripe figs."

"*Tu m'dis pas!* And where would dat be?" asked 'Ti Joe.

"In *Monsieur Boudreaux's* yard. *Tu tiens d'y aller?*" asked the *loup-garou.*

"*Mais, bien sûr!* What time will you come for me?" asked 'Ti Joe.

bien fâché (bee-yehn fah shay)—very angry
Boudreaux (boo dro)—Cajun family name

"*De bon matin. À cinq heures,*" replied the *loup-garou.*
The next morning that *canaille cochon* got up *à quatre heures* and went to *Monsieur Boudreaux's* yard, climbed that tree, and began picking those good, ripe figs, when . . . *ooh! la!* . . . he looked down and saw that *loup-garou* staring up at him.

À quatre heures (ah kot-er)—at four o'clock
ooh la—a Cajun yell or howling

"Aha! 'Ti Cochon! So you got here before me again!" the *loup-garou* called out. "Aren't doz ripe and *bonnes manger!?*"

"*Ça c'est très bon!* Would you like a taste?" asked 'Ti Joe.

With that he threw a fig as far as he could and the *loup-garou* had to run to catch it before it smashed on the ground.

As soon as the *loup-garou* turned to get the fig, 'Ti Joe jumped down from that tree and ran for his life till he reached home, safe and sound.

bonnes manger (bohn mohn zhay)—good eating
Ça c'est très bon (sah say tray bohn)—it is very good

The next day, the *loup-garou* came knocking at 'Ti Joe's door again.

"'Ti Cochon, I know dat crawfish festival is tomorrow. *Tu tiens d'y aller?*" he asked.

"*Mais, bien sûr!* And what time would you come for me?" asked 'Ti Joe.

"*Le grand midi,*" answered the *loup-garou*.

"*C'est bien.* I'll be ready," said 'Ti Joe.

Le grand midi (ler grohn mee dee)—12 noon

The next day that *canaille cochon* went to the crawfish festival *à onze heures*, had his fill of crawfish dishes, bought a new crawfish boiling pot, and started for home. Coming over *le coteau*, he saw that *loup-garou* on his way to the festival.

à onze heures (ah onz-er)—at eleven o'clock
le coteau (ler ko toe)—the hill

In a terrible fright, 'Ti Joe jumped into his new boiling pot to hide. Well, that pot did not stay still. It rolled down *le coteau*.

When the *loup-garou* looked up and saw that pot coming straight for him, oh *yie, yie!* He turned and ran all the way home!

yie, yie (y-eye, y-eye)—a Cajun expression meaning "oh, my!"

Later that day the *loup-garou* went back to 'Ti Joe's house and knocked on the door!

"'Ti Cochon! I got a terrible fright on my way to the festival today. Dis big round ting came rolling down *le coteau* at me and almost made *coosh coosh* out of me!" the *loup-garou* called out.

"Ah yee! You *bétasse loup-garou!* Dat was me in dat crawfish boiling pot!" laughed 'Ti Joe.

*coosh coosh (koosh koosh)—fried cornmeal served with
   warm milk and sugar (a good Cajun supper)*
bétasse (bay-tahs)—dumb, foolish

Hearing that, the *loup-garou* went into a rage and yelled out, "Look out now! I'm coming down dat chimney right now to eat you!"

"*Allons,*" invited 'Ti Joe, as he opened the lid of his brand new boiling pot. Down the chimney came the *loup-garou*, right into the pot!

'Ti Joe slammed the lid on real tight and cooked that *loup-garou* till he was just tender enough.

Allons (ah lohn)—come on

The next morning, 'Ti Joe was very surprised when his two *frères* knocked at his door. They were just in time for a very special breakfast of *grillades* and grits. 'Ti Joe just had to tell his brothers about the secret ingredient that made those *grillades très bon!*

Then *les trois cochons* all sat down together and had *un bon appétit!*

C'est tout!

frères (frairs)—brothers
grillades (gree ahdz)—meat and gravy served over grits (a good Cajun breakfast)
très bon (tray bohn)—very good
un bon appétit (uhn bohn ah-pah-tee)—a good meal
(say too)—that's all

'Ti Joe's Special Recipe:

GRILLADES AND GRITS

2 lb. beef or pork (wolf is acceptable)
Salt, garlic powder, and cayenne to taste
2 tbsp. flour
2 tbsp. cooking oil

1 cup chopped onions
1 tbsp. minced garlic
1 large ripe tomato (chopped)
1 cup water
3 cups cooked grits

Trim fat from meat and season meat to taste with salt, garlic powder, and cayenne pepper. Rub flour over meat. Brown the meat *(les grillades)* in oil in a large iron skillet. Brown both sides. Remove meat and add onions and garlic. Cook until onions are clear and soft, then add tomatoes and water. You may add more water if the gravy is too thick. Return meat to gravy and simmer for 45 minutes or until meat is tender. Serve over hot grits for a good Cajun breakfast.

Bon appétit, mes amis!